The Herding Clin
& Journal

Laura De La Cruz

For information, contact
The Take Pen
Laura De La Cruz
75 County Road A074
Chaparral, NM 88081
thetakepen@gmail.com

Dedication

For my good friend Narita Siegel of Narita Farms Australian Shepherds (http://www.naritafarmsaussies.com/)

MY INFORMATION

Name: _____

Dog Name: _____

Contact Information: _____

Clinics I have attended:

_____

_____

_____

_____

_____

How to use this workbook

Going to herding clinics can be overwhelming – so much going on and so easy to get overwhelmed!

This workbook/journal is designed to help you remember the lessons you learn at clinics and hopefully improve as you go along.

It includes areas for you to track:

- Which dog you took

- Who was the clinician?

- How was the facility? What did you like/dislike?

- How was the livestock? What did you like/dislike?

- How was the weather? Was it a factor?

- A space to diagram the training area

- Lots of room for notes

- An area to document the lessons you learned.

- A final decision on "loved it/hated it" for future reference!

Date: _____

Dog's Name: _____

Clinician: _____

Facility: _____

_____

Stock: _____

_____

Weather: _____

Training Area Layout

Notes

Notes

Lessons Learned

_____

_____

_____

_____

_____

_____

_____

_____

_____

_____

_____

_____

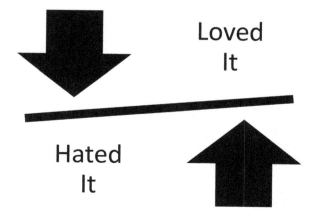

Loved
It

Hated
It

Date: _____

Dog's Name: _____

Clinician: _____

Facility: _____

_____

Stock: _____

_____

Weather: _____

Training Area Layout

Notes

Notes

Lessons Learned

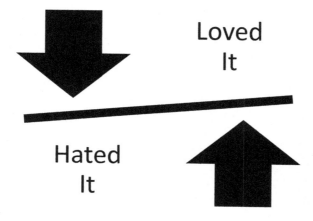

Loved It

Hated It

Date: _____

Dog's Name: _____

Clinician: _____

Facility: _____

_____

Stock: _____

_____

Weather: _____

Training Area Layout

Notes

Notes

Lessons Learned

_____

_____

_____

_____

_____

_____

_____

_____

_____

_____

_____

_____

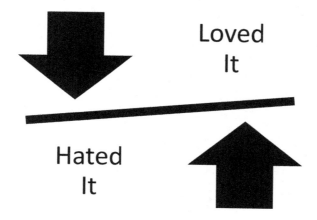

Loved It

Hated It

Date: _____

Dog's Name: _____

Clinician: _____

Facility: _____

_____

Stock: _____

_____

Weather: _____

Training Area Layout

Notes

Notes

Lessons Learned

_____

_____

_____

_____

_____

_____

_____

_____

_____

_____

_____

_____

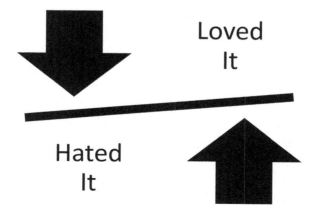

Loved
It

Hated
It

Date: _____

Dog's Name: _____

Clinician: _____

Facility: _____

_____

Stock: _____

_____

Weather: _____

Training Area Layout

Notes

Notes

Lessons Learned

_____

_____

_____

_____

_____

_____

_____

_____

_____

_____

_____

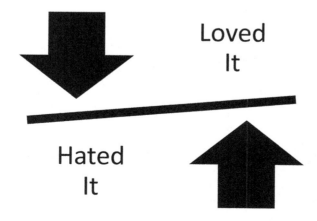

Loved
It

Hated
It

Date: ———

Dog's Name: _____

Clinician: _____

Facility: _____

_____

Stock: _____

_____

Weather: _____

Training Area Layout

Notes

Notes

Lessons Learned

_____

_____

_____

_____

_____

_____

_____

_____

_____

_____

_____

_____

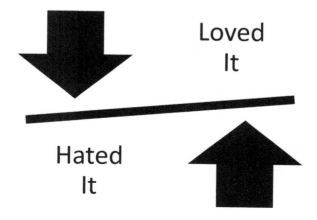

Loved
It

Hated
It

Date: ――――

Dog's Name: _____

Clinician: _____

Facility: _____

_____

Stock: _____

_____

Weather: _____

Training Area Layout

Notes

Notes

Lessons Learned

_____

_____

_____

_____

_____

_____

_____

_____

_____

_____

_____

_____

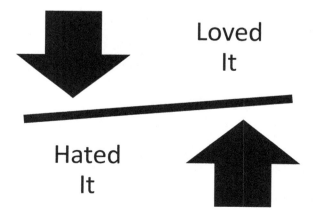

Loved
It

Hated
It

Date: _____

Dog's Name: _____

Clinician: _____

Facility: _____

_____

Stock: _____

_____

Weather: _____

Training Area Layout

Notes

Notes

Lessons Learned

_____

_____

_____

_____

_____

_____

_____

_____

_____

_____

_____

_____

_____

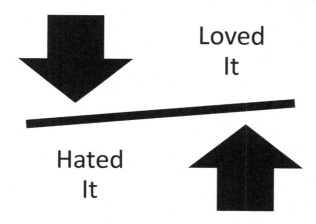

Loved
It

Hated
It

Date: _____

Dog's Name: _____

Clinician: _____

Facility: _____

_____

Stock: _____

_____

Weather: _____

Training Area Layout

Notes

Notes

Lessons Learned

_____

_____

_____

_____

_____

_____

_____

_____

_____

_____

_____

_____

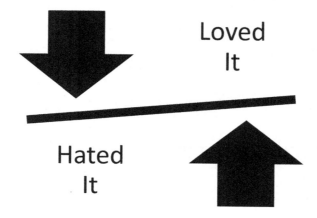

Loved
It

Hated
It

Date: _____

Dog's Name: _____

Clinician: _____

Facility: _____

_____

Stock: _____

_____

Weather: _____

Training Area Layout

Notes

Notes

Lessons Learned

_____

_____

_____

_____

_____

_____

_____

_____

_____

_____

_____

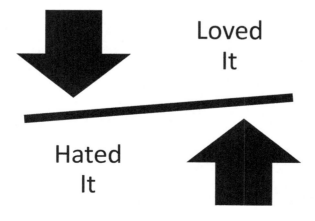

Loved
It

Hated
It

Date: _____

Dog's Name: _____

Clinician: _____

Facility: _____

_____

Stock: _____

_____

Weather: _____

Training Area Layout

Notes

Notes

Lessons Learned

_____

_____

_____

_____

_____

_____

_____

_____

_____

_____

_____

_____

_____

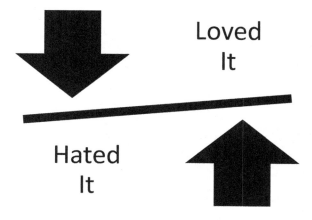

Loved
It

Hated
It

Date: _____

Dog's Name: _____

Clinician: _____

Facility: _____

_____

Stock: _____

_____

Weather: _____

Training Area Layout

Notes

Notes

Lessons Learned

_____

_____

_____

_____

_____

_____

_____

_____

_____

_____

_____

_____

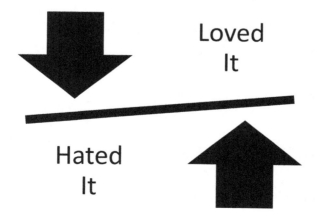

Loved
It

Hated
It

Date: _____

Dog's Name: _____

Clinician: _____

Facility: _____

_____

Stock: _____

_____

Weather: _____

Training Area Layout

Notes

Notes

Lessons Learned

_____

_____

_____

_____

_____

_____

_____

_____

_____

_____

_____

_____

_____

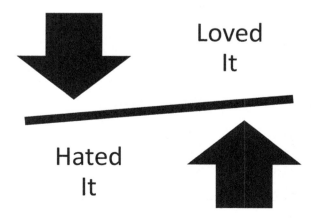

Loved
It

Hated
It

Date: _____

Dog's Name: _____

Clinician: _____

Facility: _____

_____

Stock: _____

_____

Weather: _____

Training Area Layout

Notes

Notes

Lessons Learned

_____

_____

_____

_____

_____

_____

_____

_____

_____

_____

_____

_____

_____

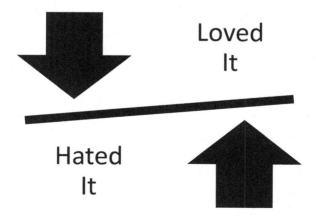

Loved
It

Hated
It

Date: _____

Dog's Name: _____

Clinician: _____

Facility: _____

_____

Stock: _____

_____

Weather: _____

Training Area Layout

Notes

Notes

Lessons Learned

_____

_____

_____

_____

_____

_____

_____

_____

_____

_____

_____

_____

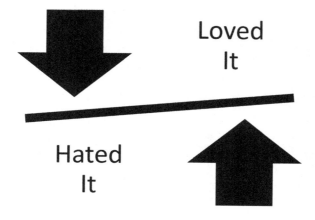

Loved It

Hated It

Thank you for buying this book!

If you liked this book, please leave a review on Amazon!

If you didn't like this book, please email me at thetakepen@gmail.com and tell me why!

If you are interested in herding lessons, or sending your dog here for lessons, please let us know! We are located in sunny Southern NM, outside of El Paso, Texas.

Look for my other books on Amazon:

"Aussie Herding – Interviews with Top Australian Shepherd Stockdog Trainers"

"The Herding Resource Book – Tips, Advice and Suggestions for People Learning to Herd with their Dogs"

"Herding Training Workbook and Journal"

"Herding Trial Workbook and Journal"

"Herding Book Journal – A Log of Books Read and Lessons Learned"

"Livestock Tracking Journal"

"Leash Up and Dig In"

Made in the USA
Middletown, DE
02 March 2019